Managing Editor
Karen Goldfluss, M.S. Ed.

Editor-in-Chief
Sharon Coan, M.S. Ed.

Art Director
CJae Froshay

Art Coordinator
Kevin Barnes

Imaging
Alfred Lau
James Edward Grace

Product Manager
Phil Garcia

Publisher
Mary D. Smith, M.S. Ed.

Numbers

GRADES 1&2

Authors

Teacher Created Resources Staff

Teacher Created Resources, Inc.
6421 Industry Way
Westminster, CA 92683
www.teachercreated.com
ISBN-13: 978-0-7439-3309-4
ISBN-10: 0-7439-3309-5
©2002 Teacher Created Resources, Inc.
Reprinted, 2006
Made in U.S.A.

Table of Contents

The old adage "practice makes perfect" can really hold true for your child and his or her education. The more practice and exposure your child has with concepts being taught in school, the more success he or she is likely to find. For many parents, knowing how to help your children can be frustrating because the resources may not be readily available. As a parent it is also difficult to know where to focus your efforts so that the extra practice your child receives at home supports what he or she is learning in school.

This book has been designed to help parents and teachers reinforce basic skills with their children. *Practice Makes Perfect* reviews basic math skills for children in grades 1 and 2. The math focus is on numbers. While it would be impossible to include all concepts taught in grades 1 and 2 in this book, the following basic objectives are reinforced through practice exercises. These objectives support math standards established on a district, state, or national level. (Refer to the Table of Contents for the specific objectives of each practice page.)

- counting to 10
- counting to 100
- counting by two's (skip counting)
- writing numbers in order
- identifying and writing ordinal numbers

- identifying sets
- comparing numbers (greater than, less than, equal to)
- counting tens and ones (place value)
- writing numbers in word form
- practicing place value (identifying hundreds, tens, and ones)

There are 32 practice pages organized sequentially, so children can build their knowledge from more basic skills to higher-level math skills. (**Note:** Have children show all work where computation is necessary to solve a problem. For multiple choice responses on practice pages, children can fill in the letter choice or circle the answer.) Following the practice pages are five practice tests. These provide children with multiple-choice test items to help prepare them for standardized tests administered in schools. As your child completes each test, he or she should fill in the correct bubbles on the answer sheet (page 46). To correct the test pages and the practice pages in this book, use the Answer Key provided on pages 47 and 48.

How to Make the Most of This Book

Here are some useful ideas for optimizing the practice pages in this book:

- Set aside a specific place in your home to work on the practice pages. Keep it neat and tidy with materials on hand.
- Set up a certain time of day to work on the practice pages. This will establish consistency. An alternative is to look for times in your day or week that are less hectic and conducive to practicing skills.
- Keep all practice sessions with your child positive and constructive. If the mood becomes tense, or you and your child are frustrated, set the book aside and look for another time to practice with your child.
- Help with instructions if necessary. If your child is having difficulty understanding what to do or how to get started, work through the first problem with him or her.
- Review the work your child has done. This serves as reinforcement and provides further practice.
- Allow your child to use whatever writing instruments he or she prefers. For example, colored pencils can add variety and pleasure to drill work.
- Pay attention to the areas in which your child has the most difficulty. Provide extra guidance and exercises in those areas. Allowing children to use drawings and manipulatives, such as coins, tiles, game markers, or flash cards, can help them grasp difficult concepts more easily.
- Look for ways to make real-life applications to the skills being reinforced.

Practice 1

Color the correct number of stars in each row.

0	☆ ☆ ☆ ☆ ☆ ☆ ☆ ☆ ☆ ☆
1	☆ ☆ ☆ ☆ ☆ ☆ ☆ ☆ ☆ ☆
2	☆ ☆ ☆ ☆ ☆ ☆ ☆ ☆ ☆ ☆
3	☆ ☆ ☆ ☆ ☆ ☆ ☆ ☆ ☆ ☆
4	☆ ☆ ☆ ☆ ☆ ☆ ☆ ☆ ☆ ☆
5	☆ ☆ ☆ ☆ ☆ ☆ ☆ ☆ ☆ ☆
6	☆ ☆ ☆ ☆ ☆ ☆ ☆ ☆ ☆ ☆
7	☆ ☆ ☆ ☆ ☆ ☆ ☆ ☆ ☆ ☆
8	☆ ☆ ☆ ☆ ☆ ☆ ☆ ☆ ☆ ☆
9	☆ ☆ ☆ ☆ ☆ ☆ ☆ ☆ ☆ ☆
10	☆ ☆ ☆ ☆ ☆ ☆ ☆ ☆ ☆ ☆

 #3309 Practice Makes Perfect: Numbers

Practice 2

To get to the gingerbread house, write the missing numerals from 0 to 100.

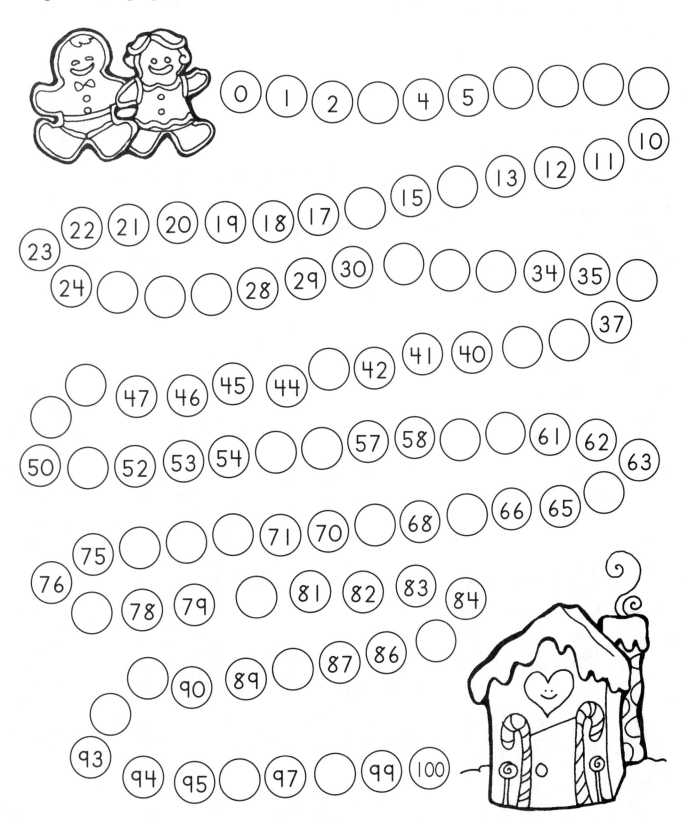

Practice 3

1. Count by 2's.

2, 4, ____ , 8,

10, ____

2. Count by 2's.

14, ____ , ____ ,

20, 22

3. Count by 2's.

24, ____ , 28,

____ , 32

4. Count the pairs of gloves. Write the number of gloves under each pair.

____ ____ ____ ____

5. Count the wheels on each bike. Write the number of wheels under each bike.

____ ____ ____ ____

6. Count by 5's.

5, 10, ____ ,

20, ____

7. Count by 5's.

30, ____ , 40,

____ , 50

8. Count by 5's.

55, 60, ____ ,

70, ____

9. Count the tally marks. (Each bundle is worth 5.)

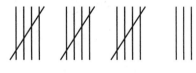

_____ tally marks in all.

10. Count the tally marks. (Each bundle is worth 5.)

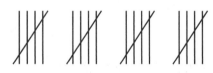

_____ tally marks in all.

Practice 4

1. Find the missing number.

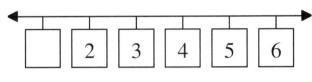

(A) 7   (B) 11   (C) 1   (D) 9

2. Find the missing number.

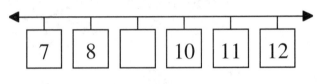

(A) 9   (B) 2   (C) 10   (D) 6

3. Find the missing number.

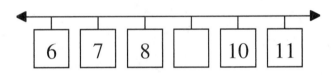

(A) 1   (B) 9   (C) 8   (D) 4

4. Find the missing number.

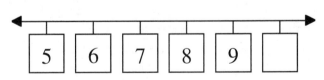

(A) 3   (B) 11   (C) 10   (D) 12

5. Find the missing number.

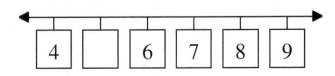

(A) 5   (B) 10   (C) 2   (D) 6

Practice 5

Write the correct numeral in each blank.

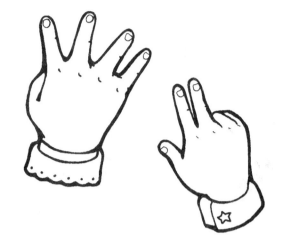

1. 3, 4, 5, _____

2. 9, 10, _____

3. 14, 15, _____

4. 21, 22, _____

5. 31, 32, _____

6. 36, _____, 38

7. 40, _____, 42

8. 47, _____, 49

9. 50, _____, 52

10. _____, 57, 58

11. 74, 75, _____

12. 80, _____, 82

13. 89, 90, _____

14. 98, _____, 100

15. 98, 99, _____

In the space below, make up some of your own counting puzzles.

Practice 6

1. Count backward. Write the missing numbers.

   12, 11, _____, 9, _____, 7, _____

2. Count backward. Write the missing numbers.

   12, _____, 10, 9, _____

3. Count backward. Write the missing numbers.

   12, _____, 10, _____, 8, _____

4. Count backward. Write the missing numbers.

   8, 7, 6, _____, _____, 3, 2

5. Count backward. Write the missing numbers.

   9, _____, _____, 6, 5

6. Count backward. Write the missing numbers.

   7, _____, 5, _____, 3

7. Count backward. Write the missing numbers.

   8, _____, _____, 5, _____

Practice 7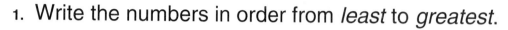

1. Write the numbers in order from *least* to *greatest*.

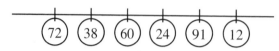

____ ____ ____ ____ ____ ____

2. Write the numbers in order from *least* to *greatest*.

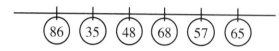

____ ____ ____ ____ ____ ____

3. Write the numbers in order from *least* to *greatest*.

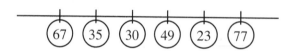

____ ____ ____ ____ ____ ____

4. Write the numbers in order from *least* to *greatest*.

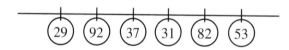

____ ____ ____ ____ ____ ____

5. Write the numbers in order from *least* to *greatest*.

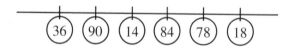

____ ____ ____ ____ ____ ____

6. Write the numbers in order from *least* to *greatest*.

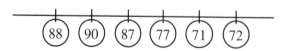

____ ____ ____ ____ ____ ____

Practice 8

1. What number comes just after 831?

   (A) 834   (B) 833   (C) 832   (D) 831

2. What number comes between 378 and 380?

   (A) 378   (B) 381   (C) 377   (D) 379

3. What number comes just before 479?

   (A) 478   (B) 475   (C) 477   (D) 476

4. What number comes just after 139?

   (A) 141   (B) 139   (C) 142   (D) 140

5. What number comes between 721 and 723?

   (A) 722   (B) 721   (C) 720   (D) 724

6. What number comes just before 400?

   (A) 398   (B) 397   (C) 396   (D) 399

7. What number comes just after 631?

   (A) 634   (B) 632   (C) 633   (D) 631

8. What number comes between 807 and 809?

   (A) 808   (B) 806   (C) 810   (D) 807

9. What number comes just before 819?

   (A) 817   (B) 816   (C) 815   (D) 818

10. What number comes just after 272?

   (A) 272   (B) 275   (C) 273   (D) 274

Practice 9

Cut out the sun, moon, and star picture boxes on page 39. Use the pictures in the space below to help you decide which comes first, second, and third in each of the problems on page 13. Then, finish the sentence on this page.

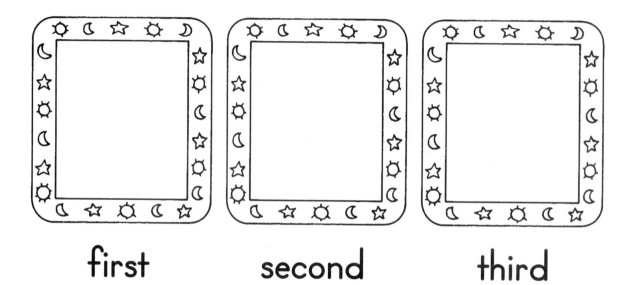

first   second   third

My favorite shape is the

Practice 9

1

The star is first.

The sun is second.

The moon is third.

2

The moon is first.

The sun is second.

The star is third.

3

The sun is third.

The star is first.

The moon is second.

4

The moon is third.

The star is second.

The sun is first.

5

The sun is first.

The moon is third.

The star is second.

6

The star is third.

The moon is first.

The sun is before the star.

7

The sun is first.

The star is next.

The moon is after the star.

8

The star is first.

The moon is last.

The sun is after the star and before
    the moon.

9

The sun is last.

The star is before the sun.

The moon is before the star.

10

The sun is first.

The star is last.

The moon is after the sun and
    before the star.

Practice 10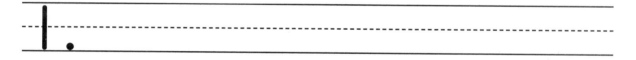

Cut out the hippo, giraffe, panda, and kangaroo picture boxes on page 39. Use the pictures in the space below to help you decide which comes first, second, and third, and fourth (last) in each of the problems on page 15. Then, write your own problem on this page.

first	**second**	**third**	**fourth**

Write your own problem.

1.

2.

3.

4.

Practice 10

1

The hippo is first.
The giraffe is second.
The panda is third.
The kangaroo is last.

2

The kangaroo is first.
The hippo is second.
The giraffe is third.
The panda is last.

3

The giraffe is first.
The kangaroo is third.
The hippo is not last.
The panda is after the kangaroo.

4

The panda is first.
The kangaroo is last.
The hippo is not third.
The giraffe is before the kangaroo.

5

The panda is third.
The giraffe is after the panda.
The kangaroo is before the panda.
The hippo is before the kangaroo.

6

The kangaroo is second.
The panda is third.
The giraffe is after the panda.
The hippo is before the kangaroo.

7

The giraffe is last.
The kangaroo is first.
The panda is after the kangaroo.
The hippo is before the giraffe.

8

The giraffe is second.
The panda is before the giraffe.
The kangaroo is last.
The hippo is after the giraffe.

9

The hippo is first.
The panda is last.
The giraffe is before the panda.
The kangaroo is before the giraffe.

10

The kangaroo is first.
The panda is third.
The giraffe is last.
The hippo is before the panda.

Practice 11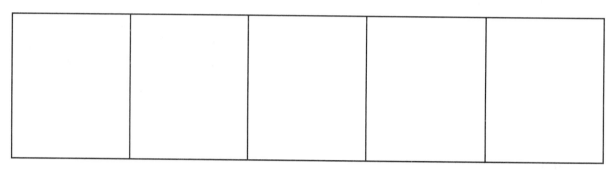

Cut out the car, train, bus, plane, and sailboat picture boxes on page 39. Use the pictures in the space below to help you decide which comes first, second, third, fourth, and fifth in each of the problems on page 17. Then, write your own problem on this page.

first   second   third   fourth   fifth

Write your own problem.

1.

2.

3.

4.

5.

    © *Teacher Created Resources, Inc.*

Practice 11

1

The sailboat is first.
The plane is last.
The bus is in the middle.
The car is after the bus.
The train is before the bus.

2

The car is first.
The train is last.
The bus is before the train.
The sailboat is second.
The plane is in the middle.

3

The car is third.
The sailboat is two places after the car.
The plane is two places before the car.
The train is second.
The bus is next to last.

4

The bus is second.
The train is before the bus.
The sailboat is last.
The car is third.
The plane is before the sailboat.

5

The plane is first.
The bus is two places after the plane.
The car is in between the plane and the bus.
The train is last.
The sailboat is after the bus.

6

The train is last.
The sailboat is before the train.
The bus is two places before the sailboat.
The car is before the sailboat.
The plane is before the bus.

7

The car is fourth.
The train is three places before the car.
The sailboat is after the train.
The bus is not last.
The plane is after the car.

8

The sailboat is fourth.
The train is after the sailboat.
The car is first.
The plane is not third.
The bus is after the plane.

9

The plane is fourth.
The train is first.
The bus is after the plane.
The sailboat is not second.
The car is before the sailboat.

10

The sailboat is fourth.
The train is after the sailboat.
The plane is before the sailboat.
The bus is not first.
The car is first.

Practice 12

1. Which shape is eighth?

 (A)   (B)   (C)   (D)

2. Which shape is third?

(A)   (B)   (C)   (D)

3. Which shape is sixth?

(A)   (B)   (C)   (D)

4. Which shape is fourth?

(A)   (B)   (C)   (D)

Practice 13

A set is a group of things with something in common, such as color, size, shape, or type of thing. Color the things that belong in each set.

Practice 14

Equivalent sets have the same number of members in both sets. Write the number in each set. Then color the two sets that have the same number of things.

1.

How many? _____

2.

How many? _____

3.

How many? _____

4.

How many? _____

Practice 15

Circle things to show equivalent sets.

1.

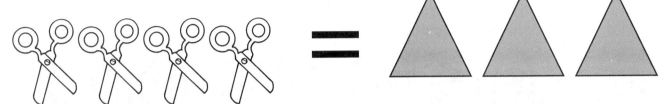

2.

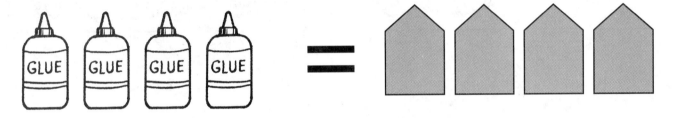

3.

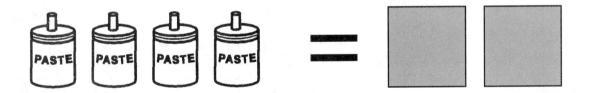

4.

Practice 16

Write the correct less than or greater than symbol between the two numbers.

< is the symbol for less than

> is the symbol for greater than

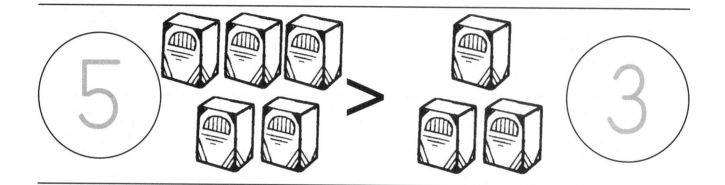

1. 10 ◯ 8   **2.** 2 ◯ 0   **3.** 35 ◯ 14

4. 64 ◯ 51   **5.** 9 ◯ 11   **6.** 79 ◯ 97

7. 5 ◯ 6   **8.** 21 ◯ 24   **9.** 100 ◯ 12

10. 25 ◯ 17   **11.** 30 ◯ 34   **12.** 80 ◯ 75

13. 15 ◯ 10   **14.** 62 ◯ 70   **15.** 14 ◯ 10

Practice 17

Draw >, <, **or** = in each box.

1.

2.

3.

4.

5.

Practice 18

Draw **>, <, or =** in each box to make each number sentence true.

1.    [ ]

2. 3   [ ]   3

3.    [ ]   5

4. 7   [ ]   11

5. 12   [ ]   10

6.    [ ]

Practice 19

1. Write >, <, or = in the circle.

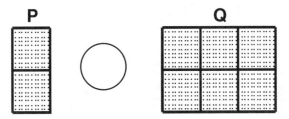

2. Write >, <, or = in the circle.

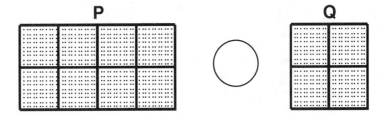

3. Write >, <, or = in the circle.

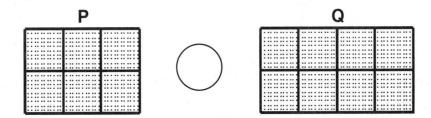

4. Write >, <, or = in the circle.

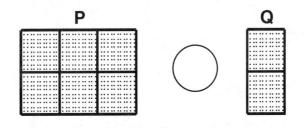

Practice 20

1. Choose <, >, or =.   (A) =   (B) >   (C) <

84 ◯ 38

---

2. Choose <, >, or =.   (A) <   (B) >   (C) =

46 ◯ 44

---

3. Choose <, >, or =.   (A) <   (B) =   (C) >

71 ◯ 15

---

4. Choose <, >, or =. Write the correct sign on the line.

18 ◯ 34   _____

---

5. Choose <, >, or =. Write the correct sign on the line.

56 ◯ 15   _____

---

6. Choose <, >, or =. Write the correct sign on the line.

94 ◯ 96   _____

Practice 21

1. Choose <, >, or =.

    87 ◯ 78

(A) =   (B) >   (C) <

2. Choose <, >, or =.

    19 ◯ 14

(A) >   (B) <   (C) =

3. Choose <, >, or =.

    59 ◯ 94

(A) =   (B) <   (C) >

4. Choose <, >, or =.

    16 ◯ 31

(A) >   (B) <   (C) =

5. Choose <, >, or =.

    72 ◯ 20

(A) =   (B) >   (C) <

6. Choose <, >, or =.

    34 ◯ 45

(A) =   (B) >   (C) <

7. Choose <, >, or =.

    39 ◯ 43

(A) <   (B) >   (C) =

8. Choose <, >, or =.

    31 ◯ 47

(A) =   (B) >   (C) <

9. Choose <, >, or =.

    23 ◯ 57

(A) <   (B) =   (C) >

10. Choose <, >, or =.

    55 ◯ 91

(A) <   (B) =   (C) >

Practice 22

1. 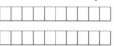 = 10 squares   (A) 80   (B) 70   (C) 7   (D) 77

How many squares?

2. □□□□□□□□□□ = 10 squares   (A) 2   (B) 22   (C) 20   (D) 30

How many squares?

3. □□□□□□□□□□ = 10 squares   (A) 90   (B) 88   (C) 80   (D) 8

How many squares?

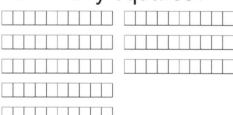

4. □□□□□□□□□□ = 10 squares   (A) 6   (B) 66   (C) 60   (D) 70

How many squares?

Practice 23

1. ☐☐☐☐☐☐☐☐☐☐ = 10 squares

How many squares?

☐☐☐☐☐☐☐☐☐☐ ☐☐☐☐☐☐☐☐☐☐
☐☐☐☐☐☐☐☐☐☐ ☐☐☐☐☐☐☐☐☐☐
☐☐☐☐☐☐☐☐☐☐ ☐☐☐☐☐☐☐☐☐☐
☐☐☐☐☐☐☐☐☐☐ ☐☐☐☐☐☐☐☐☐☐
☐☐☐☐☐☐☐☐☐☐

_____

2. ☐☐☐☐☐☐☐☐☐☐ = 10 squares

How many squares?

☐☐☐☐☐☐☐☐☐☐ ☐☐☐☐☐☐☐☐☐☐
☐☐☐☐☐☐☐☐☐☐ ☐☐☐☐☐☐☐☐☐☐
☐☐☐☐☐☐☐☐☐☐ ☐☐☐☐☐☐☐☐☐☐
☐☐☐☐☐☐☐☐☐☐
☐☐☐☐☐☐☐☐☐☐

_____

3. ☐☐☐☐☐☐☐☐☐☐ = 10 squares

How many squares?

☐☐☐☐☐☐☐☐☐☐ ☐☐☐☐☐☐☐☐☐☐
☐☐☐☐☐☐☐☐☐☐ ☐☐☐☐☐☐☐☐☐☐
☐☐☐☐☐☐☐☐☐☐
☐☐☐☐☐☐☐☐☐☐
☐☐☐☐☐☐☐☐☐☐

_____

4. ☐☐☐☐☐☐☐☐☐☐ = 10 squares

How many squares?

☐☐☐☐☐☐☐☐☐☐
☐☐☐☐☐☐☐☐☐☐
☐☐☐☐☐☐☐☐☐☐
☐☐☐☐☐☐☐☐☐☐
☐☐☐☐☐☐☐☐☐☐

_____

5. ☐☐☐☐☐☐☐☐☐☐ = 10 squares

How many squares?

☐☐☐☐☐☐☐☐☐☐
☐☐☐☐☐☐☐☐☐☐

_____

6. ☐☐☐☐☐☐☐☐☐☐ = 10 squares

How many squares?

☐☐☐☐☐☐☐☐☐☐
☐☐☐☐☐☐☐☐☐☐
☐☐☐☐☐☐☐☐☐☐
☐☐☐☐☐☐☐☐☐☐

_____

Practice 24

1. Find the number *ninety-two*.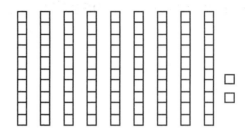

   (A) 28   (B) 93   (C) 29   (D) 92

2. Find the number *thirty-one*.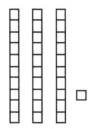

   (A) 14   (B) 31   (C) 13   (D) 32

3. Find the number *seventy-three*.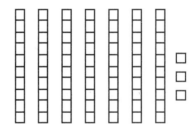

   (A) 37   (B) 36   (C) 72   (D) 73

4. Find the number *eighty-one*.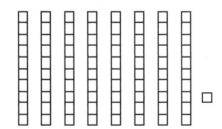

   (A) 81   (B) 17   (C) 18   (D) 80

Practice 25

1. Which number matches the blocks?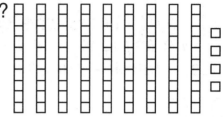

    (A) 95   (B) 49   (C) 94   (D) 50

2. Which number matches the blocks?

    (A) 22   (B) 31   (C) 23   (D) 32

3. Which number matches the blocks?

    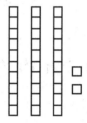

    (A) 35   (B) 52   (C) 34   (D) 53

4. Which number matches the blocks?

    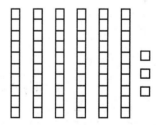

    (A) 63   (B) 64   (C) 36   (D) 37

5. Which number matches the blocks?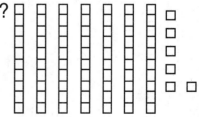

    (A) 67   (B) 77   (C) 66   (D) 76

Practice 26

Count how many tens ▯ and ones ▫. Write the number of each in the boxes. Write the number on the line.

1.

tens	ones

_____

2.

tens	ones

_____

3.

tens	ones

_____

4.

tens	ones

_____

5.

tens	ones

_____

6.

tens	ones

_____

7.

tens	ones

_____

8.

tens	ones

_____

9.

tens	ones

_____

10.

tens	ones

_____

Practice 27

Read how many tens and ones. Write the number on the line.

1. 2 tens 6 ones _____   6. 5 tens 4 ones _____

2. 3 tens 1 one _____   7. 8 tens 4 ones _____

3. 6 tens 8 ones _____   8. 9 tens 2 ones _____

4. 7 tens 5 ones _____   9. 1 ten 6 ones _____

5. 4 tens 9 ones _____   10. 4 tens 7 ones _____

Draw a line to match the pictures with the tens ☐ and ones ☐ .

11. 5 tens 2 ones   A.

12. 3 tens 1 one   B.

13. 7 tens 9 ones   C.

14. 2 tens 5 ones   D.

15. 6 tens 3 ones   E.

16. 4 tens 8 ones   F.

17. 1 ten 6 ones   G.

18. 4 tens 2 ones   H.

Practice 28

 = 10    = 1

Write the number each group of moths and silkworms represents.

1.    = _____

2.   = _____

3.    = _____

4.    = _____

5.    = _____

6. 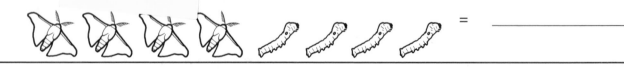   = _____

Practice 29

1. Which number has 1 ten?

   (A) 191   (B) 149   (C) 419   (D) 491

---

2. Which number has 4 ones?

   (A) 425   (B) 640   (C) 245   (D) 254

---

3. Which number has 7 tens?

   (A) 807   (B) 737   (C) 780   (D) 870

---

4. Which number has 5 tens?

   (A) 456   (B) 465   (C) 546   (D) 565

---

5. Look at the number below.

   ### 35**8**

   Is the **bolded** digit in one's, ten's, or hundred's place?_____

---

6. Look at the number below.

   ### 7**9**8

   Is the **bolded** digit in one's, ten's, or hundred's place? _____

Practice 30 ଽ ଓ ଽ ଓ ଽ ଓ ଽ ଓ ଽ ଓ ଽ ଓ ଽ ଽ ଓ

1. Which number has 8 tens?

   (A) 832　　　　(B) 382　　　　(C) 828　　　　(D) 328

2. Which number has 2 tens?

   (A) 282　　　　(B) 216　　　　(C) 162　　　　(D) 126

3. Which number has 9 ones?

   (A) 739　　　　(B) 793　　　　(C) 991　　　　(D) 973

4. Which number has 6 hundreds?

   (A) 296　　　　(B) 269　　　　(C) 964　　　　(D) 629

5. Which number has 5 hundreds?

   (A) 655　　　　(B) 587　　　　(C) 875　　　　(D) 857

6. Find the number that has 8 tens, 6 hundreds, and 5 ones.

   (A) 685　　　　(B) 190　　　　(C) 658　　　　(D) 568

7. Find the number that has 0 tens, 9 hundreds, and 5 ones.

   (A) 590　　　　(B) 905　　　　(C) 140　　　　(D) 950

8. Find the number that has 8 tens, 6 hundreds, and 3 ones.

   (A) 170　　　　(B) 683　　　　(C) 368　　　　(D) 638

Practice 31

1. What is the number in word form?

3 tens and 5 ones

(A) fifty-three   (B) three-ten five

(C) three hundred five   (D) thirty-five

2. What is the number in word form?

4 tens and 5 ones

_____

3. What is the number in word form?

5 tens and 6 ones

_____

4. What is the number in word form?

7 tens and 9 ones

(A) seventy-nine   (B) seven hundred nine

(C) ninety-seven   (D) seven-ten nine

5. What is the number in word form?

5 tens and 2 ones

_____

Practice 32

1. What is the number in word form?

   2 hundreds, 9 tens, and 8 ones

   (A) nine-hundred ninety-eight   (B) two-hundred ninety-eight
   (C) nine hundred eight   (D) two-hundred eighty-nine

2. What is the number in word form?

   7 tens and 8 ones

   (A) seven hundred eight   (B) eighty-seven
   (C) seven-ten eight   (D) seventy-eight

3. What is the number in word form?

   3 hundreds, 2 tens, and 6 ones

   (A) three-hundred sixty-two   (B) three hundred twenty-six
   (C) two hundred six   (D) two-hundred sixty-three

4. Write the number in word form.

   9 tens and 7 ones_____

5. Write the number in word form.

   2 hundreds, 7 tens, and 2 ones_____

6. Write the number in word form.

   3 tens and 2 ones_____

Picture Boxes

(NOTE: Picture boxes appear on page 40 so that cut outs have images on both sides.)

Use with pages 12 and 13.

Use with pages 14 and 15.

Use with pages 16 and 17.

Picture Boxes

Test Practice 1

1. Find the missing number.

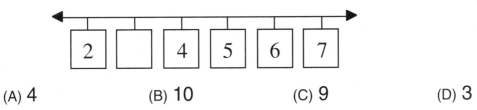

(A) 4   (B) 10   (C) 9   (D) 3

2. Find the missing number.

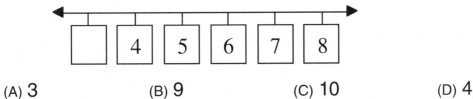

(A) 3   (B) 9   (C) 10   (D) 4

3. Choose the sign to use in the circle.   (A) <   (B) =   (C) >

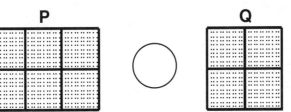

4. If you hang the number tags in order from *least* to *greatest, which number will be second?*

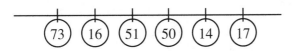

(A) 51   (B) 50   (C) 16   (D) 17

5. Which shape is eighth?

(A)   (B)   (C) ☆   (D) △

Test Practice 2

1. Choose the sign to make the problem correct.

   74 ◯ 61

   (A) =   (B) <   (C) >

2. Choose the sign to make the problem correct.

   94 ◯ 47

   (A) <   (B) =   (C) >

3. What is the number in word form?

   2 tens and 4 ones

   (A) forty-two   (B) twenty-four

   (C) two hundred four   (D) two-ten four

4. What is the number in word form?

   4 tens and 9 ones

   (A) four hundred nine   (B) forty-nine

   (C) ninety-four   (D) four-ten nine

5. Which number matches the blocks?

   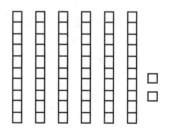

   (A) 26   (B) 62   (C) 63   (D) 27

Test Practice 3

1. Find the number *seventy-four*.

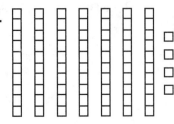

  (A) 73   (B) 48   (C) 47   (D) 74

2. Find the number *ninety-two*.

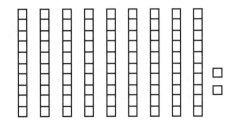

  (A) 92   (B) 28   (C) 93   (D) 29

3. What number comes between 75 and 77?

  (A) 74   (B) 78   (C) 76   (D) 75

4. What number comes just before 397?

  (A) 393   (B) 396   (C) 394   (D) 395

5. 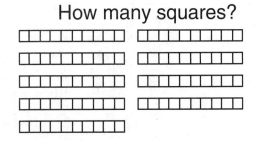 = 10 squares

How many squares?

  (A) 9   (B) 90   (C) 100   (D) 99

Test Practice 4

Choose the correct answer to solve the problem. If the answer is not given, choose "none of these."

---

1. Which number has 8 tens?

Ⓐ 872

Ⓑ 285

Ⓒ 368

Ⓓ none of these

---

2. Which number has 7 ones?

Ⓐ 721

Ⓑ 407

Ⓒ 178

Ⓓ none of these

---

3. Which number is the same as 8 tens and 5 ones?

Ⓐ 158

Ⓑ 58

Ⓒ 85

Ⓓ none of these

---

4. Choose the sign to use in the circle.

Ⓐ >

Ⓑ <

Ⓒ =

Ⓓ none of these

---

5. Name the eleventh letter in this sentence.

Sam likes to play basketball.

Ⓐ p

Ⓑ o

Ⓒ l

Ⓓ none of these

---

6. What is the seventh number in this series?

2   0   1   4   9   3   8   5   6   7

Ⓐ 3

Ⓑ 5

Ⓒ 9

Ⓓ none of these

---

7. What is the number 95 in word form?

Ⓐ fifty-nine

Ⓑ ninety-five

Ⓒ nine-hundred fifty

Ⓓ none of these

Test Practice 5

Choose the correct answer to solve the problem. If the answer is not given, choose "none of these."

---

1. If these numbers are written in order from least to greatest, which number will be fourth?

7   3   5   9   12   10

- Ⓐ 7
- Ⓑ 10
- Ⓒ 9
- Ⓓ none of these

---

2. Find the missing numbers.

3, _____, _____, 6, _____, 8

- Ⓐ 2, 4, 7
- Ⓑ 4, 5, 7
- Ⓒ 5, 7, 9
- Ⓓ none of these

---

3. Find the missing numbers.

12, 14, _____, 18, _____, _____, 24

- Ⓐ 16, 22, 23
- Ⓑ 15, 20, 22
- Ⓒ 16, 21, 23
- Ⓓ none of these

---

4. How many stars should be added on the left to make the sets equivalent?

★ ★ ★ ★ ★
★ ★ ★ ★ ★   =   ★ ★ ★ ★ ★ ★
★ ★ ★ ★ ★   ★ ★ ★ ★ ★ ★
                 ★ ★ ★ ★ ★ ★

- Ⓐ 4
- Ⓑ 6
- Ⓒ 3
- Ⓓ none of these

---

5. Which number has 8 tens?

- Ⓐ 280
- Ⓑ 208
- Ⓒ 820
- Ⓓ none of these

---

6. Which number has 5 hundreds?

- Ⓐ 452
- Ⓑ 354
- Ⓒ 534
- Ⓓ none of these

---

7. Find the number one-hundred twenty-one.

- Ⓐ 120
- Ⓑ 102
- Ⓒ 221
- Ⓓ none of these

Answer Sheet

Test Practice 1	Test Practice 2	Test Practice 3
1. Ⓐ Ⓑ Ⓒ Ⓓ	1. Ⓐ Ⓑ Ⓒ	1. Ⓐ Ⓑ Ⓒ Ⓓ
2. Ⓐ Ⓑ Ⓒ Ⓓ	2. Ⓐ Ⓑ Ⓒ	2. Ⓐ Ⓑ Ⓒ Ⓓ
3. Ⓐ Ⓑ Ⓒ Ⓓ	3. Ⓐ Ⓑ Ⓒ Ⓓ	3. Ⓐ Ⓑ Ⓒ Ⓓ
4. Ⓐ Ⓑ Ⓒ Ⓓ	4. Ⓐ Ⓑ Ⓒ Ⓓ	4. Ⓐ Ⓑ Ⓒ Ⓓ
5. Ⓐ Ⓑ Ⓒ Ⓓ	5. Ⓐ Ⓑ Ⓒ Ⓓ	5. Ⓐ Ⓑ Ⓒ Ⓓ

Test Practice 4	Test Practice 5	NOTE
1. Ⓐ Ⓑ Ⓒ Ⓓ	1. Ⓐ Ⓑ Ⓒ Ⓓ	
2. Ⓐ Ⓑ Ⓒ Ⓓ	2. Ⓐ Ⓑ Ⓒ Ⓓ	
3. Ⓐ Ⓑ Ⓒ Ⓓ	3. Ⓐ Ⓑ Ⓒ Ⓓ	
4. Ⓐ Ⓑ Ⓒ Ⓓ	4. Ⓐ Ⓑ Ⓒ Ⓓ	
5. Ⓐ Ⓑ Ⓒ Ⓓ	5. Ⓐ Ⓑ Ⓒ Ⓓ	
6. Ⓐ Ⓑ Ⓒ Ⓓ	6. Ⓐ Ⓑ Ⓒ Ⓓ	
7. Ⓐ Ⓑ Ⓒ Ⓓ	7. Ⓐ Ⓑ Ⓒ Ⓓ	

NOTE

Use of this Answer Sheet is optional. A child can simply circle or fill in the letters of the correct answers on the practice pages. When ready, he or she can then practice filling in the bubbles on this page by transferring the responses to the appropriate test page boxes.

Answer Key

Page 4

0	☆ ☆ ☆ ☆ ☆ ☆ ☆ ☆ ☆ ☆
1	★ ☆ ☆ ☆ ☆ ☆ ☆ ☆ ☆ ☆
2	★ ★ ☆ ☆ ☆ ☆ ☆ ☆ ☆ ☆
3	★ ★ ★ ☆ ☆ ☆ ☆ ☆ ☆ ☆
4	★ ★ ★ ★ ☆ ☆ ☆ ☆ ☆ ☆
5	★ ★ ★ ★ ★ ☆ ☆ ☆ ☆ ☆
6	★ ★ ★ ★ ★ ★ ☆ ☆ ☆ ☆
7	★ ★ ★ ★ ★ ★ ★ ☆ ☆ ☆
8	★ ★ ★ ★ ★ ★ ★ ★ ☆ ☆
9	★ ★ ★ ★ ★ ★ ★ ★ ★ ☆
10	★ ★ ★ ★ ★ ★ ★ ★ ★ ★

Page 5

Page 6

1. 6; 12
2. 16; 18
3. 26; 30
4. 2, 2, 2, 2
5. 2, 2, 2, 2
6. 15; 25
7. 35; 45
8. 65; 75
9. 18
10. 20

Page 7

1. C
2. A
3. B
4. C
5. A

Page 8

1. 6
2. 11
3. 16
4. 23
5. 33
6. 37
7. 41
8. 48
9. 51
10. 56
11. 76
12. 81
13. 91
14. 99
15. 100

Page 9

1. 10; 8; 6
2. 11; 8
3. 11; 9; 7
4. 5; 4
5. 8; 7
6. 6; 4
7. 7; 6; 4

Page 10

1. 12, 24, 38, 60, 72, 91
2. 35, 48, 57, 65, 68, 86
3. 23, 30, 35, 49, 67, 77
4. 29, 31, 37, 53, 82, 92
5. 14, 18, 36, 78, 84, 90
6. 71, 72, 77, 87, 88, 90

Page 11

1. C
2. D
3. A
4. D
5. A
6. D
7. B
8. A
9. D
10. C

Page 13

1. star, sun, moon
2. moon, sun, star
3. star, moon, sun
4. sun, star, moon
5. sun, star, moon
6. moon, sun, star
7. sun, star, moon
8. star, sun, moon
9. moon, star, sun
10. sun, moon, star

Page 15

1. hippo, giraffe, panda, kangaroo
2. kangaroo, hippo, giraffe, panda
3. giraffe, hippo, kangaroo, panda
4. panda, hippo, giraffe, kangaroo
5. hippo, kangaroo, panda, giraffe
6. hippo, kangaroo, panda, giraffe
7. kangaroo, panda, hippo, giraffe
8. panda, giraffe, hippo, kangaroo
9. hippo, kangaroo, giraffe, panda
10. kangaroo, hippo, panda, giraffe

Page 17

1. sailboat, train, bus, car, plane
2. car, sailboat, plane, bus, train
3. plane, train, car, bus, sailboat
4. train, bus, car, plane sailboat
5. plane, car, bus, sailboat, train
6. plane, bus, car, sailboat, train
7. train, sailboat, bus, car, plane
8. car, plane, bus, sailboat, train
9. train, car, sailboat, plane, bus
10. car, bus, plane, sailboat, train

Page 18

1. B
2. C
3. B
4. A

Page 19

1. Color all but tennis racket and ball.
2. Color all but four-sided shape.
3. Color all but triangle.
4. Color all but umbrella.

Page 20

1. 5
2. 4
3. 4
4. 3

Color sets in #2 and #3.

Page 21

1. Circle any three scissors and all three triangles.
2. Circle all in each side.
3. Circle any two paste jars and both squares.
4. Circle all on each side.

Page 22

1. >
2. >
3. >
4. >
5. <
6. <
7. <
8. <
9. >
10. >
11. <
12. >
13. >
14. <
15. >

Page 23

1. =
2. >
3. <
4. >
5. >

Answer Key

Page 24
1. >
2. =
3. <
4. <
5. >
6. <

Page 25
1. <
2. >
3. <
4. >

Page 26
1. B
2. B
3. C
4. <
5. >
6. <

Page 27
1. B
2. A
3. B
4. B
5. B
6. C
7. A
8. C
9. A
10. A

Page 28
1. B
2. C
3. C
4. C

Page 29
1. 90
2. 80
3. 70
4. 50
5. 20
6. 40

Page 30
1. D
2. B
3. D
4. A

Page 31
1. C
2. D
3. A
4. A
5. D

Page 32
1. 2, 3, 23
2. 4, 8, 48
3. 8, 4, 84
4. 3, 6, 36
5. 1, 9, 19
6. 5, 7, 57
7. 6, 5, 65
8. 9, 1, 91
9. 4, 4, 44
10. 5, 2, 52

Page 33
1. 26
2. 31
3. 68
4. 75
5. 49
6. 54
7. 84
8. 92
9. 16
10. 47
11. E
12. G
13. H
14. D
15. B
16. C
17. F
18. A

Page 34
1. 32
2. 50
3. 25
4. 42
5. 44
6. 19

Page 35
1. C
2. D
3. D
4. A
5. one's place
6. ten's place

Page 36
1. B
2. D
3. A
4. D
5. B
6. A
7. B
8. B

Page 37
1. D
2. forty-five
3. fifty-six
4. A
5. fifty-two

Page 38
1. B
2. D
3. B
4. ninety-seven
5. two hundred seventy-two
6. thirty-two

Page 41
1. D
2. A
3. C
4. C
5. D

Page 42
1. C
2. C
3. B
4. B
5. B

Page 43
1. D
2. A
3. C
4. B
5. B

Page 44
1. B
2. B
3. C
4. B
5. A
6. D
7. B

Page 45
1. C
2. B
3. D
4. C
5. A
6. C
7. D